MW00898148

HIDDEN WORLDS
THE GREEKS
and TROY

by Deborah Tyler

 DILLON PRESS
New York

First American publication 1993 by Dillon Press,
Macmillan Publishing Company, 866 Third Avenue,
New York, NY 10022

Macmillan Publishing Company is part of the
Maxwell Communication Group of Companies.

First published in Great Britain
by Zoë Books Limited

A ZOË BOOK

Devised and produced by
Zoë Books Limited
15 Worthy Lane
Winchester
Hampshire SO23 7AB
England

j938
9T981
1993

Printed in Italy by Grafedit SpA
Design: Jan Sterling, Sterling Associates
Picture research; Suzanne Williams
Illustrations: Francis Phillipps
Map: Gecko Limited
Production: Grahame Griffiths

10 9 8 7 6 5 4 3 2 1

Library of Congress Cataloging-in-Publication Data

Tyler, Deborah.
    The Greeks and Troy / by Deborah Tyler.
      p. cm — (Hidden worlds)
    Includes bibliographical references and index.
    Summary: Describes the historic city of Troy
through discoveries made by Heinrich Schliemann
and others.
    ISBN 0-87518-537-1
    1. Greece — History — To 146 B.C. — Juvenile
literature. 2. Troy (Extinct city) — Juvenile literature.
3. Mycenae (Extinct city) — Juvenile literature.
4. Trojan War — Juvenile literature. 5. Excavations
(Archaeology) — Turkey — Troy (Extinct city) —
Juvenile literature. 6. Excavations (Archaeology) —
Greece — Mycenae (Extinct city) — Juvenile
literature. 7. Schliemann, Heinrich, 1822-1890 —
Influence — Juvenile literature. I. Title. II. Series.
    DF221.T8T95 1993
    938—dc20   93– 18693

Photographic acknowledgments
The publishers wish to acknowledge, with thanks, the
following photographic sources:

Ancient Art & Architecture Collection: front cover,
6, 27b; British Museum: 15, 21, 24t; C. M. Dixon:
title page, 18t & b, 22b, 23t & b, 24b, 26, 27t, 28;
English Heritage: 14b; Robert Harding Picture
Library: 29b; Michael Holford: 5, 8, 9, 25; Hulton
Deutsch Collection: 13t, 14t, 22t; Impact Photos: 7t /
Homer Sykes; the Mansell Collection: 12, 13b;
National Gallery: 10; Werner Forman Archive: 29t;
Zefa: 7b, 19, 20.

Contents

Introduction   4

Hissarlik   6

Tales of long ago   8

In search of Troy   10

Digging up the past   12

Examining clues   14

Troy reconstructed   16

Mycenae and Tiryns   18

Who were the Trojans?   20

How people lived   22

Crops and trade   24

War and warriors   26

Dates and ideas   28

Glossary   30

Index   32

Introduction

Turkey is a country that lies across the borders of two of the large land masses, or **continents**, of the world. Part of Turkey is in Europe and part of it is in Asia. The two continents are divided by a narrow stretch of water that links the Aegean Sea and the Black Sea. The ancient Greeks called this narrow stretch of water, or **strait**, the Hellespont. Today it is called the Dardanelles, and the chief port on its Asian shore is a town called Çanakkale.

In about 3000 B.C. a settlement grew up to the southwest of the modern town of Çanakkale, near the western entrance to the Dardanelles. For thousands of years people lived at this site. Towns were built there, and towns were destroyed.

The finest city of all stood there sometime between 1300 and 1200 B.C. The people who lived there probably collected silver or other valuable goods from the ships that passed through the strait. The settlement became smaller after

▼ The Aegean Sea lies in the eastern Mediterranean, between Europe and Asia. In ancient times it was crossed by ships from Egypt, Crete, Mycenae, and the kingdoms of western Asia.

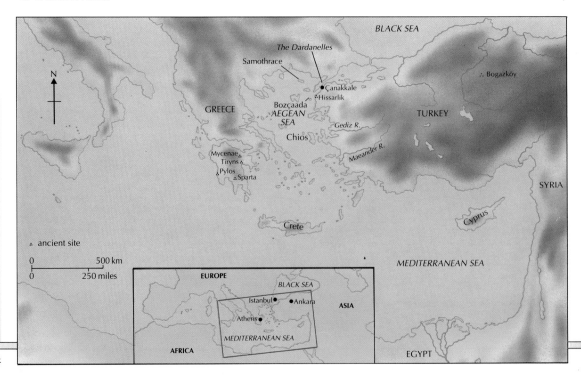

1000 B.C. The last town on the site was attacked and ruined in the year A.D. 259.

When the Turks invaded the region, they called the site Hissarlik, which means the "place of the fort." Visiting Europeans believed that Hissarlik was the site of a city made famous by the ancient Greeks. That city was known as Troy, or Ilium.

Over 3,000 years ago

At the time when the settlement at Hissarlik was at its wealthiest, **civilizations** had grown up along the shores of the Mediterranean and Aegean seas. To the south, Egypt was a land of great temples and cities, ruled by kings called pharaohs. The powerful **Hittite** kingdom stretched eastward from the Aegean Sea to the Euphrates River. In the west, Greece was made up of a number of small states. These were settlements built around fortified palaces, or **citadels**. By 1400 B.C. a people called the Mycenaeans were the most powerful force in Greece.

Hissarlik

Today visitors from Europe can cross the Dardanelles by car ferry to Çanakkale. If they drive 25 miles southwest, they come to a village called Teufikiye. This was built with stones taken from the ruins of Hissarlik. Cotton fields cover the surrounding plain.

The mound of Hissarlik rises above the flat countryside. It drops about 32 feet on its steep northern and western sides. The site is overgrown with bushes, but signposts guide visitors around the ditches and ruined walls. Some of these are more than 13 feet thick.

People of long ago would not recognize the site today. There are no fine buildings still standing. The landscape has changed. The natural shape of the mound has been altered by digging.

▼ Was this ancient Troy? Today only ruined walls and stones stand at Hissarlik.

Even the ancient harbor, by which the city once made its living, has disappeared.

Over thousands of years the harbor **silted** up. Shipping channels became blocked. A hundred years ago visitors described the area as a marsh. Since then it has turned into dry land.

Ancient Troy?

These days most people believe that Hissarlik is the site of Troy. They imagine Greek warriors sailing across the blue waters of the Aegean Sea and landing on the beaches. They look across the dusty plain and imagine the Greeks in their **bronze** armor, riding up in their **chariots** to **besiege** the city walls.

For thousands of years people have tried to prove that Troy was built here. For all that time, the mound at Hissarlik has been at the center of a fascinating historical detective story.

▲ The Dardanelles separate Europe from Asia. Countless armies have crossed these straits from the days of the ancient Greeks until the 20th century.

▼ The Dardands gate at Hissarlik

Tales of long ago

▶ We know very little about Homer, the poet. He is first mentioned by Greek historians, such as Herodotus, who lived a long time after Homer's death. The Greeks believed that Homer composed the *Iliad*, the marvelous story of the siege of Troy. They also believed that he composed the *Odyssey*, which tells about the adventures of the Greeks after the Trojan War. Some said that Homer was born in the eastern Aegean on the island of Chios and that he was blind.

The ancient Greeks told many stories about Troy. One concerned Helen, who was said to be the most beautiful woman in the world. She married Menelaus, king of Sparta, a state in Greece. King Priam of Troy had a son named Paris. Paris went to stay in Sparta and fell in love with Helen. When Menelaus had to go to the island of Crete, Helen ran away with Paris to Troy.

In his fury Menelaus asked his brother Agamemnon for help. He was king of another Greek state, Mycenae. Agamemnon raised an army to help fight the people of Troy, called Trojans. The aim was to bring back Helen to her husband. It took the Greeks ten years to win this Trojan war.

Everyone was thrilled by the tale, for it told the deeds of heroes such as Achilles and Hector, of the noble women who lived at Troy, and of the gods and goddesses of ancient Greece.

Poems about Troy

The story of Troy remains famous thousands of years later. At first the tales were told in public by storytellers, people who told stories as a way of making a living. These storytellers learned the words by heart, but sometimes they changed the details. The tale was told as a poem. The rhythm and the rhymes of poetry made the words easier to remember. Later the story was written down and copied by hand.

The best surviving poem about Troy is the oldest. It is called the *Iliad*. We are not sure who wrote the *Iliad*, but it is said to have been the work of a Greek named Homer. He may have lived in about 800 B.C. The events in the poem took place hundreds of years before Homer was alive. He could only have heard about the Trojan War from other storytellers.

Was it fact or fiction? Everyone who read the *Iliad* wondered if there really had been a city called Troy. Had the Trojans fought the Greeks, and if so, when? How could people find out?

▼ This Greek vase was made in 490 B.C. The decoration shows the climax of the story told in the *Iliad*. Achilles and Hector fight to the death. Achilles, wearing a helmet, shield, and sword, lunges forward with his spear to kill Hector.

In search of Troy

▲ The story of the *Iliad* continued to fascinate Europeans in the Middle Ages. Some royal families even claimed descent from the heroes of Troy. In the fifteenth and sixteenth centuries, **scholars** became very interested in ancient Greece and Rome. This painting by Fra Angelico shows Helen being carried away by Paris and his men.

The first people who tried to solve the mystery of the Trojan War studied the words of the *Iliad*. Homer's long poem did not state exactly where the ancient city had been built. However, the poem offered some clues.

The *Iliad* said that Troy stood on a windy plain. The poem described how the gods watched a battle between the Greeks and Trojans from a mountain on the island of Samothrace. It also said that the Greek army camped on an island called Bozcaada. Visitors to Hissarlik today can see both these places from the mound.

Exploring the region

About 2,000 years ago, a geographer named Strabo toured ancient Greece and Turkey, and wrote about the landscape that he saw. His guidebook was used by later travelers exploring the region around Hissarlik. One of these was an Italian scholar, Cyriacus of Ancona. He wrote notes about the region (which he believed to be Troas, the land around ancient Troy) about 500 years ago.

By the 1700s it was fashionable for rich people in western Europe to collect ancient coins and sculptures. This encouraged travellers to search for the sites of ancient cities.

In 1750 an Englishman named Robert Wood wrote about his travels in the region. Wood's book was so popular that it was translated into four languages. Just over 100 years later, Frank Calvert, an Englishman who lived in Turkey, bought some land at Hissarlik. He began the first dig to find out what was in the mound.

▼ An English poet named Alexander Pope began to translate the *Iliad* in 1715. This map shows what Pope thought the site of ancient Troy looked like.

Digging up the past

▲ An engraving of the hill at Hissarlik in the 1870s, when Schliemann started his excavations

The search for Troy started in earnest. Digs, or **excavations**, at Hissarlik began to uncover ancient walls. Objects that had been made long ago, or **artifacts**, were discovered at the site.

The study of ancient remains is called **archaeology**. Scientific methods of examining ancient remains began to be introduced toward the end of the nineteenth century. Until then people dug for treasure, for personal gain, or for curiosity. Unfortunately, this meant that many ancient sites were damaged long before any scientific investigations had begun.

Schliemann's dream

In 1870 a German named Heinrich Schliemann came to Hissarlik. Schliemann was a man with a single dream. He wanted to prove that Homer's city of Troy had really existed. He was fascinated by the *Iliad* and was sure that the Trojan War was

◀ Heinrich Schliemann was born in Germany in 1822. He worked as a businessman in Holland and Russia, and became very rich. He retired at the age of 36 and spent the rest of his life trying to prove that Homer's stories were about events that really happened. Few scholars believed him. However, his excavations were successful, and he made many exciting discoveries.

▼ Heinrich Schliemann's wife, Sophie, was photographed wearing Trojan jewelry that had been buried at Hissarlik. Schliemann called the necklaces and earrings "Helen's jewels." No one knows where they are now.

not a story, or **legend**, but a real event in history.

Schliemann wanted to find the remains under the mound. He knew what he was looking for, but he had little idea what it would look like. He was in charge of six excavations at Hissarlik between 1870 and 1890. At times there were as many as 100 workmen on the site. They dug through many layers of remains until they found the oldest stones. It seemed that, at various periods in history, a new city had been built on top of the ruins of the previous settlement.

For twenty years Schliemann tried to unlock the secrets of Hissarlik. He believed that all the finds at the site were connected with the *Iliad*. He did not realize that he had dug right through to the earliest settlement, which dated from 1,000 years *before* the likely date of the Trojan War.

Examining clues

▶ Schliemann's first excavations at Hissarlik were carried out using unscientific methods. Later work was carried out by Wilhelm Dörpfeld, one of the best archaeologists of his day.

When Heinrich Schliemann died in 1890, his assistant Wilhelm Dörpfeld continued the work. Dörpfeld had trained to be an **architect**, a person who designs buildings. This training helped him to get a better idea of the layout of the old buildings by looking at the stones and ditches of Hissarlik.

In the 1930s an American scholar named Carl Blegen spent six years at Hissarlik. The earlier digs had destroyed many important clues. Blegen used new methods to study what was left. By now archaeology had become a science. The days of the treasure hunters were over.

▼ Computers can sort information very quickly and store detailed records. Archaeologists may also use magnetometers, which measure the strength of magnetism in the earth, to **survey** a particular site. This picture of a ditched enclosure was built up from a magnetometer survey.

Uncovering the past

Today when archaeologists excavate a site, they look for more than very beautiful or very old objects. They examine every clue to the past, including tiny fragments of broken pottery or fabric. These fragments often contain enough clues to tell archaeologists where the artifact was made and who made it. The age of the artifact can tell them when people lived at the site. For example, Dörpfeld discovered pottery at Hissarlik that was made by the Mycenaean Greeks. This proved that there was contact between the Mycenaeans and the settlement at Hissarlik.

Archaeologists take care not to damage the surroundings. They survey the site to study the lay of the land. They plan the **grids** and the lines of the **trenches** with the greatest care. Soil must be scraped or brushed away by hand and then put through a sieve. Experts try to figure out what the buildings would have looked like when they were still standing. Stones may have been removed before the ruins were buried by soil.

Examining the evidence

Once objects have been uncovered they must be kept for **analysis**. They may be treated with chemicals, **X-rayed**, or taken away for **radiocarbon dating**. Analysis of the remains of plants will give clues about the climate and the supply of food at the site being excavated. Analysis has told us, for instance, that there was probably a **famine** in the Aegean region around 1200 B.C. Analysis of samples of soil has confirmed that there was once a harbor at Hissarlik.

▼ Today's archaeologists can use many methods that were unknown in the days of Schliemann. Carbon is found in all natural substances, such as bones, cloth, and plants. Carbon is also radioactive, and once the natural substance has died, the radioactivity of the carbon begins to reduce, or decay. Machines like this one at the British Museum can figure out the age of an object containing carbon by measuring the amount of this decay. This is called radiocarbon dating.

Troy reconstructed

As Carl Blegen dug through the layers of soil at Hissarlik, he gave numbers to the various settlements that he uncovered. Troy I, the earliest settlement, dated from about 3000 B.C. Troy II dated from about 2300 B.C. Troy II was a citadel built of mud bricks and timber on stone foundations.

A golden age

Troy VI was the name that Blegen gave to the settlement in the period after 1300 B.C. At this level he found the foundations of walls and some ruins. The stonework that remained was of such high quality that Blegen decided this must have been the wealthiest settlement on the site. Over 9,000 gold artifacts were found at Hissarlik. Heinrich Schliemann discovered silver jewelry and bronze daggers. This city had been one of the richest in the Aegean.

▼ Archaeology helps to rebuild past worlds. This picture shows Troy VI, the wealthiest city ever built at Hissarlik, as it may have looked over 3,200 years ago.

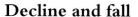

Decline and fall

Archaeologists believe that Troy VI was destroyed by an earthquake. After the earthquake the city walls were repaired. Troy VII was built on the rubble; but instead of grand houses and wide streets, there were now poor houses huddled closely together. This city was eventually burned to the ground, and the great days of the settlement were over.

In about 700 B.C. the Greeks founded a new **colony** at Hissarlik, called New Ilium. It became a small market town. The last town on the site is called Troy IX by archaeologists. Troy IX was built by the Romans and destroyed in A.D. 259 by fierce **Goths** from northern Europe.

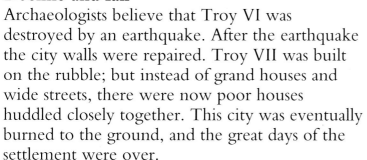

Mycenae and Tiryns

Hissarlik is just one piece in the great Trojan puzzle. Heinrich Schliemann soon realized that the full story would never be known until sites on the Greek mainland were also excavated. It was from the Greek mainland that the warriors left to attack Troy. It was also on the Greek mainland that stories such as the *Iliad* were passed on from one generation to the next.

Golden graves

Schliemann decided to dig at Mycenae, the state once ruled by King Agamemnon. The *Iliad* described him as the "king of men," the most powerful ruler of the Greek states. There was no problem finding the site, for, unlike Troy, the name of Mycenae had never changed. It was still marked on the maps of the day.

Schliemann expected to find evidence of a wealthy palace at Mycenae. The stone walls of

▲ Was this the face of Agamemnon, the king of Mycenae who led the Greeks to Troy? Heinrich Schliemann believed it was, but it has now been dated to an earlier period. It seems that the Mycenaeans, like the Egyptians, placed gold masks on the faces of rulers when they died.

▶ The graves at Mycenae contained wonderful treasures. They provide a key to our understanding of the ancient Aegean civilizations.

the citadel at Mycenae were entered through a magnificent gate guarded by stone lions. The walls surrounded the remains of a palace that dated from the thirteenth century B.C. In 1876 Schliemann uncovered **shaft graves** that were full of treasure. He was most excited by a mask made of gold. He called it the "Mask of Agamemnon." Later archaeologists found that it dated from about 1500 B.C., about 300 years before the time of the great king.

Tiryns

In 1884 Schliemann excavated the site of another ancient citadel near Mycenae called Tiryns. With Dörpfeld, he found the remains of a palace with strong walls. Like the one at Mycenae, it was built on a site that was easy to defend. The buildings were of stone, including fine marble. Both citadels had a good water supply, and enough corn grew nearby to feed many people.

◀ This picture shows part of a vaulted gallery built into the walls at the citadel of Tiryns. The strong walls built around the palaces of the Aegean at this time tell us that wars were common. The city could be attacked at any time.

Who were the Trojans?

Some of the Trojan mysteries remain unsolved. What did the people of Hissarlik call their own city? What language did they speak? Who were these "Trojans"?

History is often written by the people who win wars rather than by the people who lose them. If the Greeks did win a Trojan War, they would have wanted to keep that memory alive. That might explain why most of our information about the Trojans comes from the Greeks. However, archaeologists also found some interesting new clues about the Trojans in Turkey.

The Hittites and Troy

In 1906 a German scholar named Hugo Winckler and a Turkish archaeologist named Theodore Makridi excavated a citadel at Bogazköy, in Turkey. This site was found to be ancient Hattushash, capital city of the great Hittite

▶ In 1834 a Frenchman named Charles Texier wrote about his visits to the ancient site of Bogazköy. Fifty years later Archibald Henry Sayce, an English professor, studied Texier's notes. Sayce noticed links between Bogazköy and Carchemish, on the Euphrates River. He believed that they were both part of a great Bronze Age kingdom. This encouraged more excavations at Bogazköy.

kingdom. Hattushash had been a very important city in the thirteenth and fourteenth centuries B.C.

The archaeologists made an exciting find at this site. They discovered an **archive** room, full of ancient records and letters written on clay **tablets**. These tablets contained new evidence about the Trojan War.

The Hittites wrote about their powerful neighbors in the West, whom they called the *Ahhiyawa*. Homer used a similar name, *Achaioi*, for the Greeks of Mycenae. The tablets included a letter written from a Hittite emperor, Hattusilis III, to a king named Agamemnon. The letter described a war with a Greek king that had taken place on the Aegean coast. The war was fought over a place called Wilusa. Another tablet recorded a **treaty** between a king of the Hittites and a king named Aleksandrus of Wilusa. The *Iliad* refers to a Trojan prince named Alexandros. Could Wilusa and Homer's Troy be the same place as modern Hissarlik?

The clay tablets from Bogazköy suggest the Trojan War did take place. However, no Hittite objects have yet been found at Hissarlik, and archaeologists are still looking for Trojan objects in the region once ruled by the Hittites.

▲ The tablets from Bogazköy were written in two ancient languages, Akkadian and Hittite. It took a long time to understand the tablets. These tablets were important to historians because they included reports of wars on the coast of the Aegean.

How people lived

The artifacts discovered at Hissarlik, Mycenae, Tiryns, and Bogazköy tell something about everyday life in the Aegean region during the period of time known as the Bronze Age. The Bronze Age was a time in the development of civilization when bronze, a mixture of tin and copper, was used to make weapons, tools, and other items.

Life in the citadels

Most of the finds belonged to wealthy people, such as kings, princesses, priests, and noble warriors. At Mycenae, precious goods were buried alongside their owners in hidden graves. The precious goods included plates and cups, **ornate** weapons, and magnificent pieces of silver

▲ Heinrich Schliemann called these finds "the treasure of Priam." Priam was the king of Troy in the *Iliad*. The artifacts found at Hissarlik proved that the rulers of the ancient city were very wealthy. Schliemann was interested only in the more valuable finds. Many ordinary objects and fragments must have been lost or thrown away during his excavations.

▶ Wall paintings at Mycenae show women in their best clothes. Their hair is plaited and tied back. Both men and women wore rings. Women wore earrings and bracelets.

This fine bronze dagger was found in a grave at Mycenae. The dagger is decorated with silver and gold, and shows three noblemen hunting lions. Lions were still to be found in Greece during the Bronze Age.

jewelry. Gold had the highest value of all the metals. These finds tell us about the rich and important people, but we know less about the lives led by ordinary people in these palace states. There were sailors, shepherds and farmers, merchants, weavers, builders, and metal workers. We also know that slaves, who had been captured during wars, worked as **laborers** and servants. Women slaves worked in the fields.

Both Greeks and Trojans ate from deep pottery bowls. Oil and wine were stored in jars with looped handles. Kitchen tools, or **utensils**, were made from bone and metal. Because wood, leather, and fabric decay quickly, we know little about clothing or furniture from Mycenae or Troy. Some of the clay tablets recorded luxury items, such as a couch with carved legs of gold. The walls, floors, and ceilings inside the flat-roofed houses were decorated with paintings.

Writing and records

As the finds at Bogazköy showed, writing in the Aegean region was mainly used for keeping records of important events, for sending messages between rulers, or for keeping records of royal stores. The Greeks from Mycenae used a writing, or **script**, that archaeologists call **Linear B**. The symbols were scratched onto the clay tablets.

A gold seal ring from a grave at Mycenae. It shows a warrior fighting three enemies.

Crops and trade

After a meal, people clear away the scraps and throw them into garbage dumps. These dumps can provide useful clues for archaeologists. Bones found in the dumps can still be identified, even if they are thousands of years old. Wall paintings at Tiryns show duck, deer, and boar. Bones from these animals have been found at excavations of the Aegean citadels, showing that these animals must have been hunted for food.

Many other foods were eaten by the peoples

▲ Hundreds of these whorls were found at Hissarlik. The whorls were attached to a stick and whirled around and around, spinning wool into yarn that was used for weaving. Trojan women spent a lot of time spinning and weaving.

▶ Schliemann found piles of fish bones at Hissarlik. Fishermen still catch mackerel nearby. The people at Mycenae also ate fish. They painted pictures of fish and other sea creatures, like this octopus, on their pottery.

of the ancient Aegean region. Large storage jars found at Mycenae contained the remains of peas, beans, and barley. These must have been grown as crops. Tablets written in the Linear B script describe how bread was made. Women ground the flour and men made the loaves. The tablets also tell us that the food given to slaves included wheat and figs.

Not all the crops were grown for food. **Flax** plants were cultivated for their fiber, which was spun and woven into linen.

Merchants of the Aegean

The Greeks grew more grain and flax than they needed for themselves. The extra crops were exchanged with other countries for goods that the Greeks needed. The goods given in exchange are known as **exports**, and the goods received are called **imports**. Other goods exported by the Greeks included woven linen, olive oil, and pottery. Linear B tablets record the export of olive oil from Mycenae to Egypt. Ivory and silver pins from Mycenae were discovered at Hissarlik. Pottery from Mycenae has been found on the coast of modern Turkey and along the Maeander and Gediz rivers. Pottery from Troy has been found as far away as Syria, Cyprus, and Palestine.

The ancient Greeks and Trojans imported copper and tin, which were needed to make the bronze for weapons and tools. Gold and purple dyes were imported from Syria. **Amber** was imported from the Baltic region of northern Europe. Lapis lazuli, which is a deep-blue stone that is used in jewelry, was imported from distant Afghanistan.

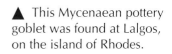

▲ This Mycenaean pottery goblet was found at Lalgos, on the island of Rhodes.

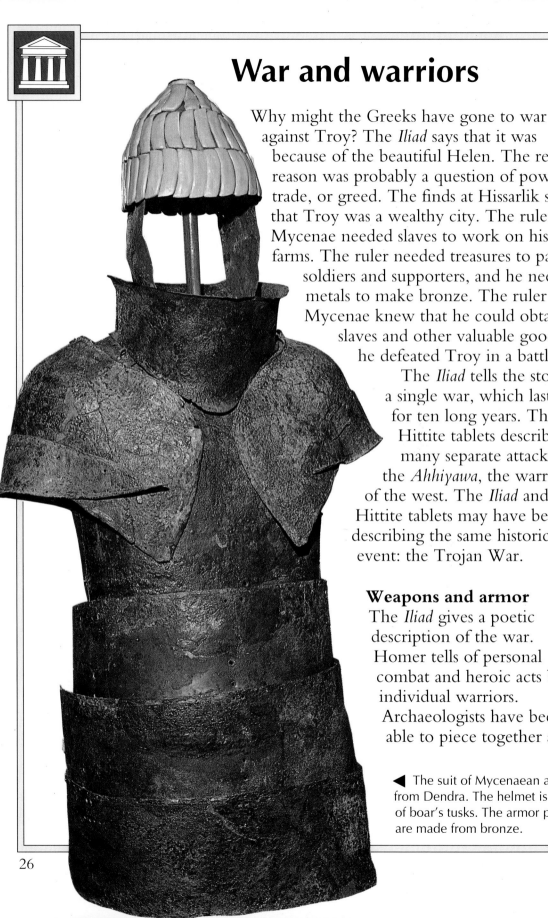

War and warriors

Why might the Greeks have gone to war against Troy? The *Iliad* says that it was because of the beautiful Helen. The real reason was probably a question of power, trade, or greed. The finds at Hissarlik show that Troy was a wealthy city. The ruler of Mycenae needed slaves to work on his farms. The ruler needed treasures to pay his soldiers and supporters, and he needed metals to make bronze. The ruler of Mycenae knew that he could obtain slaves and other valuable goods if he defeated Troy in a battle.

The *Iliad* tells the story of a single war, which lasted for ten long years. The Hittite tablets describe many separate attacks by the *Ahhiyawa*, the warriors of the west. The *Iliad* and the Hittite tablets may have been describing the same historical event: the Trojan War.

Weapons and armor

The *Iliad* gives a poetic description of the war. Homer tells of personal combat and heroic acts by individual warriors. Archaeologists have been able to piece together a

◄ The suit of Mycenaean armor from Dendra. The helmet is made of boar's tusks. The armor plates are made from bronze.

◀ This vase from Mycenae is about 3,200 years old. It is decorated with pictures of warriors from Mycenae. They are wearing helmets made from animal horns. Helmets like these were described in the *Iliad*, and one was found at Pylos, in southwest Greece.

more detailed picture. The Mycenaean Greeks would have sailed to war in a boat with a sail and long oars. The Greek warriors rode into battle on carriages, or chariots, pulled by horses but fought on foot. They were armed with long spears, swords, daggers, bows, and arrows.

Shields may have been made of animal skin, or **hide**. The hide would have been stretched over a **wicker** frame into a figure-eight shape. Warriors such as Achilles may have worn armor. A suit of armor that dates from the fifteenth century B.C. was found at Dendra, near Mycenae, in 1960. This suit would have covered a warrior's body in heavy bronze plates.

▼ A detail from a wall painting that is over 3,000 years old. It shows Greek warships in action.

Dates and ideas

▶ A detail from a vase decorated with the Wooden Horse

Archaeologists are trying to prove that a city at Hissarlik was destroyed before Mycenae and the Greek states lost their power. By studying the style of Mycenaean pottery found at Hissarlik, archaeologists believe that the earthquake which destroyed Troy VI occurred after 1300 B.C. The remains of Troy VII—the crowded settlement built on the ruins of Troy VI—show that it was probably sacked and burned between 1210 and 1180 B.C.

We know that the Greek states, including Mycenae, declined after 1200 B.C. If the Greeks did defeat the Trojans, the rout probably happened before this date. Another clue supports this idea. In Homer's story about the fall of Troy, King Nestor of Pylos is a wise old man. Archaeologists have found the ruins of a palace at Pylos that was burned about 1200 B.C. and never rebuilt. If King Nestor did fight in the Trojan War, it must have been shortly before 1200 B.C. So if Homer's Troy existed at all, it would most likely have been Troy VII at Hissarlik.

What happened to the Trojans?

Pottery finds tell us that some people survived the fire at Troy VII, but by 1100 B.C. the site was abandoned. What became of the Trojans?

Hundreds of years later the Romans claimed that *they* were descended from the Trojans. In 19 B.C., the great Roman poet Virgil wrote about the adventures of the Trojan hero Aeneas. He described how the Greeks fooled the Trojans by entering the city hidden inside a wooden horse. He claimed that, after the destruction of Troy, Aeneas traveled westward across the Mediterranean Sea. Virgil's story remains nothing more than a legend.

New ideas

The experts are still arguing about Troy and the date of the war with the Greeks. Scholars study the evidence and come up with different opinions. A new theory was published in 1992 by Eberhard Zangger, a German **geologist**. He believed that Hissarlik was the lost city of Atlantis, which had been described by a Greek named Solon over 2,500 years ago. Other scholars disagree with his views. One thing is certain. The puzzle of ancient Troy will continue to fascinate people, as it has done for thousands of years.

▲ Mycenae did not last much longer than Troy. Its citadel was abandoned about 1100 B.C. Tablets found at Ugarit, in Syria, tell of famine. Egyptian carvings from this period tell of a major attack by "sea peoples" —warriors of the eastern Mediterranean. Such events may explain the end of the Bronze Age kingdoms in the Aegean. This Egyptian carving shows Ramses II fighting against the "sea peoples."

◄ Ancient Troy or Atlantis? As more discoveries are made at Hissarlik, more questions are raised and more arguments erupt among scholars.

Glossary

amber: the fossilized resin of pine trees. It is usually dark yellow.

analysis: a detailed examination

archaeology: the scientific study of ancient remains

architect: a person who designs buildings

archive: an area where records are stored. These records are often stored for historical reasons.

artifact: any object made and used by people

besiege: to surround a town, cutting off its supplies, before attacking it

bronze: a metal made of copper mixed with tin

chariot: a vehicle with two wheels, often pulled by a horse

citadel: a well-defended building inside a city

civilization: a group of people, or society, that has made advances in government, science, or the arts

colony: a country (or part of a country) owned by another country

continent: one of the large land masses of the world, such as Africa and Asia

excavation: the place where archaeologists dig for evidence of the past

exports: goods transported out of a country, in return for other goods or payment

famine: a great lack of food in a country

flax: a plant whose fibers are woven into cloth, usually linen

geologist: a scientist who studies rocks and the structure of the earth

Goths: a group of people, or tribe, who lived in the area now called Germany. In the third, fourth, and fifth centuries A.D., they attacked and invaded much of Europe.

grid: a system of squares marked out on the ground before an archaeological excavation begins. Each square is given a number, or reference. All of the objects found by the archaeologists in one square will be labeled with that square's reference number. This means that the archaeologists can be certain where the object was found.

hide: an animal skin

Hittite: an ancient people who lived in the area now known as Anatolia (the part of Turkey within Asia) from about 1700-1180 B.C.

imports: goods transported into a country, in return for other goods or payment

laborer: a person who does a job that requires strength but little skill

legend: an old story that many people believe even though it may not be quite true

Linear B: an ancient form of writing. Linear B is similar to ancient Greek and dates from about 1400 B.C.

ornate: highly decorated

radiocarbon dating: measuring the rate of radioactive decay in an object in order to date it

scholar: a person who studies

script: a form of writing, usually ancient

shaft grave: a grave like the ones found by Schliemann at Mycenae, which were in rooms, or chambers, at the bottom of a deep, square pit, or shaft.

silted: blocked by mud or sand

strait: a narrow stretch of water

survey: to take exact measurements of the land or of a site

tablet: a piece of stone or wood on which words or symbols have been carved

treaty: an agreement, usually between two countries

trench: a long, narrow ditch cut through the ground

utensil: a tool that is used for cooking or eating

wicker: a twig, often willow

X-ray: to take photographs of the inside of an object through the outer covering by using an invisible ray

Index

Achaioi 21
Achilles 8, 9, 27
Aeneas 29
Agamemnon 8, 18, 19, 21
Ahhiyawa 21, 26
animals 23, 24
archaeology 12, 14-16
archives 21
armor 7, 9, 26, 27
artefacts 12, 14, 15, 16, 22
Blegen, Carl 14, 16
boats 4, 27
Bogazköy 20, 21, 22, 23
bread 25
bronze 7, 16, 22, 23, 25, 26, 27
Calvert, Frank 11
Çanakkale 4, 6
carbon 15
citadels 5, 16, 19, 22, 24, 29
clay tablets 21, 23, 25, 26, 29
clothing 14, 15, 22
computers 14
copper 22, 25
Crete 4, 8
Dardanelles 4, 6, 7
Dörpfeld, Wilhelm 14, 15, 19
dyes 25
Egypt 4, 5, 18, 29
excavations 12-15, 22, 24
famine 15, 29
food 15, 19, 24, 25
gold 16, 18, 19, 23, 25
grain crops 19, 25
graves 18, 19, 22, 23
Hattushash 20, 21
Hector 8, 9
Helen 8, 10, 13, 26
Herodotus 8
Hittites 5, 20-21, 26

Homer 8, 9, 10, 12, 21, 26, 28
hunting 24
Iliad 8-9, 10, 11, 12, 13, 18, 21,
    22, 26, 27
jewelry 13, 16, 22, 23, 25
Linear B 23, 25
Makridi, Theodore 20
marble 19
Menelaus 8
Mycenae 4, 5, 8, 15, 18, 19, 21-29
paintings 22, 23, 24
plants 15
Pope, Alexander 11
pottery 9, 14, 15, 23, 24, 25, 28, 29
Pylos 27, 28
radiocarbon dating 15
Sayce, Archibald 20
Schliemann, Heinrich 12-14, 15,
    16, 18, 19, 22, 24
scripts 23, 25
silver 4, 16, 22, 23, 25
slaves 23, 26
Solon 29
Strabo 11
Texier, Charles 20
tin 22, 25
Tiryns 19, 22, 24
tools 22, 25
trading 25, 26
Trojan War 8-9, 10, 12, 13, 20, 21,
    26, 28
Virgil 29
weapons 22, 25, 26-27
weaving 24, 25
Wilusa 21
Winckler, Hugo 20
Wood, Robert 11
X rays 15
Zangger, Eberhard 29